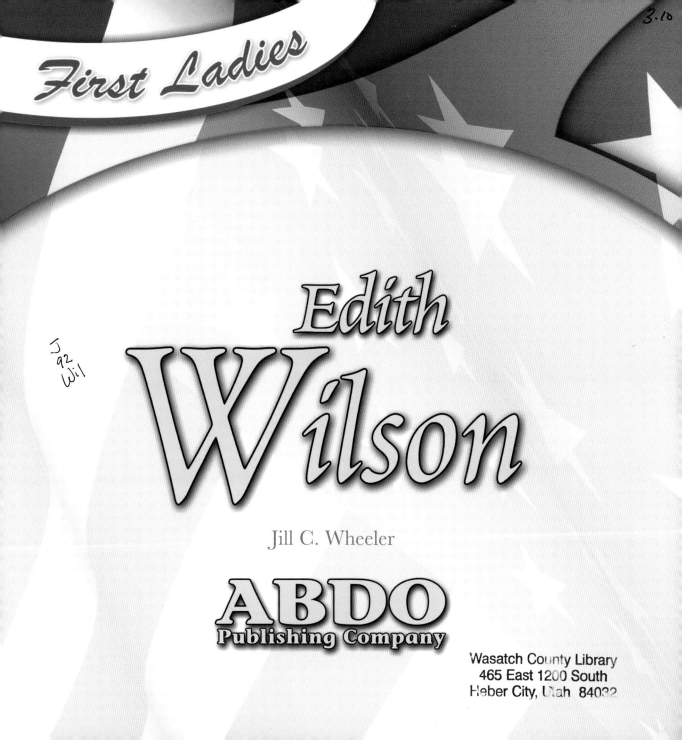

First Ladies

Edith
Wilson

Jill C. Wheeler

ABDO
Publishing Company

visit us at
www.abdopublishing.com

Published by ABDO Publishing Company, 8000 West 78th Street, Edina, Minnesota 55439.
Copyright © 2010 by Abdo Consulting Group, Inc. International copyrights reserved in all
countries. No part of this book may be reproduced in any form without written permission from the
publisher. The Checkerboard Library™ is a trademark and logo of ABDO Publishing Company.

Printed in the United States.

Manufactured with paper containing at least 10% post-consumer waste

Cover Photo: Library of Congress
Interior Photos: Alamy p. 26; Art Resource p. 5; Corbis pp. 10, 13, 14, 17, 23, 27;
 Getty Images p. 25; Library of Congress pp. 9, 11, 12, 15, 18, 19, 21;
 Woodrow Wilson House, a National Trust Historic Site, Washington, D.C. pp. 6, 7

Series Coordinator: BreAnn Rumsch
Editors: Megan M. Gunderson, BreAnn Rumsch
Art Direction & Cover Design: Neil Klinepier

Library of Congress Cataloging-in-Publication Data

Wheeler, Jill C., 1964-
 Edith Wilson / Jill C. Wheeler.
  p. cm. -- (First ladies)
 ISBN 978-1-60453-634-8
 1. Wilson, Edith Bolling Galt, 1872-1961--Juvenile literature. 2. Presidents' spouses--United
States--Biography--Juvenile literature. I. Title.

 E767.3.W63W445 2010
 973.91'3092--dc22
 [B]

       2009003039

Contents

Edith Wilson

In 1915, Edith Wilson became America's First Lady. She was the second wife of Woodrow Wilson, the twenty-eighth U.S. president. As First Lady, Mrs. Wilson gained much access to her husband's work. She attended his private meetings in the Oval Office. She even learned to read coded messages sent during **World War I**.

Mrs. Wilson is best remembered for briefly fulfilling her husband's presidential duties. President Wilson suffered a **stroke** during his second term in office. Mrs. Wilson wanted to protect her husband's position. So, she handled all of his letters and visitors. As President Wilson's **steward**, she unofficially acted as president while he recovered.

Many people later criticized Mrs. Wilson for her actions during the president's illness. However, she had no political ambition of her own. More than anything, Mrs. Wilson was devoted to her husband. Today, she remains a memorable First Lady.

Edith Wilson's companionship helped her husband face great challenges during his presidency.

Southern Childhood

Edith Bolling was born on October 15, 1872, in Wytheville, Virginia. Her parents were William and Sallie Bolling. William worked as a lawyer and a judge. Sallie was a homemaker. She cared for the large Bolling family. Edith had ten brothers and sisters!

Edith's family was related to Southern **aristocrats**. Her grandfather had been a wealthy man at one

William Bolling

Sallie Bolling

Edith (center) *was the seventh child born in the Bolling family.*

time. However, he lost all of his land during the American **Civil War**.

The Bollings lived in a maze of rooms above three street-level shops. They did not have much money. What little they did have they shared with other relatives. At some meals, there were 15 or 20 mouths to feed!

Edith's three older sisters attended the local school. However, Edith was too shy to join them. She looked to her father and grandmother for lessons instead. At home, Edith's father helped her read classic literature. Her grandmother taught her to tailor dresses, sew, and crochet.

Leaving Home

Edith was educated at home until she was 15. In 1887, she entered Martha Washington College in Abingdon, Virginia. There, she studied music and many other subjects. These included history and mathematics. However, Edith did not like the school. It was cold and she was frequently hungry. So, she left after just one year.

In 1889, Edith began attending Powell's School in Richmond, Virginia. She liked Powell's much better than Martha Washington College. Yet, the Bolling family still had Edith's three younger brothers to educate. They could not afford to keep Edith in school, too. So, she left Powell's in 1890. Edith never returned to a formal school. Years later, she wished she had received a better education.

When Edith was 18, she began visiting her older sister Gertrude in Washington, D.C. Gertrude lived there with her husband, Alexander Galt. Edith made several trips to visit them. Each time, she stayed for a few months. Edith soon met one of Alexander's cousins. His name was Norman Galt.

At Martha Washington College, students learned various sciences and languages. They also studied grammar, government, and geography.

First Love

Edith grew into a beautiful woman.

Norman came from a prominent family. The Galts owned a successful jewelry and silver business in Washington, D.C. Norman quickly fell in love with Edith. Yet at first, she was unaware of his interest.

Norman spent four years courting Edith. During that time, he visited her often and sent gifts and flowers. The two married on April 30, 1895.

After the wedding, the **newlyweds** made their home in Washington, D.C. There, Norman managed the family jewelry store. To help Edith's family, he hired three of her brothers to work there.

In 1903, Edith and Norman had a son. Sadly, the boy died as an infant. The couple never had another child. Still, they had a loving marriage. They enjoyed traveling together. Over the years they visited Ireland, Germany, and France.

Edith and Norman's life together came to an end in January 1908. Norman became ill and died. He was just 45 years old. Norman had become the owner of the jewelry store several years earlier. Now, Edith was left to run the business. She hired a manager to operate the store. But, she remained involved in many key decisions.

Norman's store, Galt and Brothers

Meeting the President

As a widow, Edith visited Europe each year. On one trip, a young woman named Alice Gordon went along. Edith had agreed to travel with her as a favor to Alice's father.

When the trip began, Edith and Alice barely knew each other. Yet during their travels, the two became close. Their friendship soon changed Edith's life forever.

Dr. Cary Grayson

Through Alice, Edith met a doctor named Cary Grayson. He was President Woodrow Wilson's doctor. After President Wilson's wife Ellen died in August 1914, Dr. Grayson wrote to Edith. He mentioned the president was beside himself with sadness.

President Wilson's cousin Helen Bones had

been close to Mrs. Wilson, too. Dr. Grayson thought Edith might be able to cheer up Helen. Edith agreed and began spending time with her.

In March 1915, Helen invited Edith to have tea at the White House. Edith went, believing the president was away playing golf. Yet, she arrived just as President Wilson returned to the White House! He was immediately entranced by her.

Before his career in politics, Woodrow Wilson had been a professor. He had also served as president of Princeton University in Princeton, New Jersey.

A New First Lady

In spring 1915, Edith began spending a lot of time with President Wilson. He invited her to the White House for dinners. Edith sailed with him on the Potomac River. The couple took automobile rides together. They also exchanged many love letters.

President Wilson had been married to his wife Ellen for nearly 30 years. After her death, he had missed having a lady companion. Now because of Edith, he was happy once again.

Still, some of President Wilson's advisers were worried. He was planning to run for reelection the following year. They feared it would look bad if the president were in love again so soon.

The wedding license for Edith and Woodrow Wilson's marriage

However, President Wilson and Edith ignored these warnings. They were in love. On December 18, 1915, they married at Edith's home in Washington, D.C. The **newlyweds** took a brief **honeymoon** to Hot Springs, Virginia. Then, Edith moved into the White House. She was ready to begin her new role as First Lady!

Edith's home in Washington, D.C.

Trusted Adviser

When Mrs. Wilson became First Lady, **World War I** was raging in Europe. The war became a focus of the 1916 presidential election. President Wilson reminded voters that he had kept the United States **neutral** in the conflict.

The First Lady also became a focus during the campaign. At first, some people criticized President Wilson's quick remarriage. Yet as Americans got to know Mrs. Wilson, they found her charming and fashionable. In the end, the First Lady did not cost President Wilson the election. He began his second term in March 1917.

Meanwhile, Mrs. Wilson had become one of her husband's most

Wartime White House

As First Lady, Mrs. Wilson was focused on supporting her husband. She was not interested in being a traditional White House hostess. Instead, she turned the White House into an example of wartime sacrifice.

After the United States entered World War I, Mrs. Wilson eliminated all official entertaining. This included White House tours, the annual Easter Egg Roll, and various receptions. Throughout the war, Mrs. Wilson did her best to support the nation. She was a patriot by example. She was also a strong First Lady for the president.

In their free time, the Wilsons enjoyed golfing and horseback riding. Mrs. Wilson also liked driving the president around Washington, D.C., in her automobile.

trusted advisers. She had access to state papers and other top secret information. President Wilson discussed important matters with her.

By 1917, President Wilson decided the United States could no longer avoid the war. On April 2, he asked Congress to declare war against Germany. Congress granted the president's request on April 6.

While President Wilson worked, Mrs. Wilson was often by his side. Soon, she learned a secret wartime code. She helped the president code and decode messages between him and his top adviser.

Supporting the War Effort

Save a loaf a week -
- Help win the war

On June 30, 1917, Mrs. Wilson registered with the U.S. Food Administration. As a member, she promised to conserve products for the war.

Mrs. Wilson quickly threw herself into aiding the American war effort. Meat, wheat products, and gasoline were all needed for the war. So, Mrs. Wilson set an example for other Americans. She limited the use of those items in the White House.

The First Lady even brought sheep to the White House. They kept the lawn cut. And later, she was able to **donate** the wool to the war effort. It earned more than $50,000.

Mrs. Wilson's sheep remained at the White House for the rest of President Wilson's term.

Mrs. Wilson knew American soldiers needed her support. She knitted trench helmets and sewed pajamas, pillowcases, and blankets. The First Lady also volunteered at the American Red Cross canteen at Union Station in Washington, D.C. There, soldiers could stop for a meal while traveling to or from war.

Privately, Mrs. Wilson helped the war effort by caring for her husband. He was under much pressure dealing with the conflict. So, she made it her job to help him relax. The two were never apart for more than a few hours each day.

Votes for Women

As First Lady, Mrs. Wilson was in a powerful position. Yet at that time, many women in the United States had little power. So they were fighting to gain suffrage, or the right to vote. The suffrage movement had started in the mid-1800s. After 1900, it had grown stronger.

Women who favored the right to vote were called suffragists. They participated in marches. One group of suffragists had even picketed the White House in January 1917. Their signs challenged President Wilson to consider giving them the right to vote.

Mrs. Wilson did not agree with the suffragists. She believed that letting women vote would upset home life for many families. Still, the First Lady had invited the protesters in from the cold. They refused, however. Many suffragists went to jail for picketing the White House.

In time, women would win the right to vote. Congress passed the Nineteenth **Amendment** to the U.S. **Constitution** in 1920. It was officially approved the same year. Throughout her life, Mrs. Wilson remained politically active. However, she never voted in a presidential election.

Suffragists picketed the White House for months, regardless of the weather.

Visiting Europe

By the end of 1918, **World War I** was drawing to a close. An **armistice** declared on November 11 stopped the fighting. Millions of people celebrated the end of this deadly war.

Next, a peace treaty needed to be written and signed. This would officially end World War I. Mrs. Wilson encouraged her husband to attend the Paris Peace Conference in France. There, he could help plan the peace treaty. President Wilson agreed to go.

Together, the Wilsons sailed for Europe. This was a first for a president's wife. No other First Lady had traveled to Europe while her husband was president. On December 13, the Wilsons arrived in France. Cheering crowds greeted them.

In Europe, the Wilsons were busy. Mrs. Wilson visited injured soldiers. She also met with queens and other royal women. With this, American First Ladies gained equal standing with European royalty.

Near the end of their trip, President Wilson gave a speech. Mrs. Wilson wanted to hear her husband speak, but only men were allowed. So, she listened from behind a curtain! Soon after, the Wilsons sailed for home.

Before leaving Europe, the Wilsons also visited England. They met with (left to right) Queen Mary, King George V, and Princess Mary.

The Secret President

Back in the United States, Mrs. Wilson's concern for her husband's health grew. She tried her best to keep him from becoming too strained. Yet, there was only so much she could do.

On October 2, 1919, President Wilson suffered a **stroke**. This left him partially **paralyzed**. Dr. Grayson told Mrs. Wilson that her husband could not handle any more pressure.

Mrs. Wilson wanted her husband to rest and get well. Yet she did not want him to lose his position as president. So, she decided to manage the details and routine duties of his job herself. Mrs. Wilson called herself the president's **steward**.

The First Lady stayed at President Wilson's side constantly. She hid how sick he was from his **cabinet** members and the public. Anyone wishing to see him needed her permission. In addition, Mrs. Wilson read all of the president's letters and papers. She decided what was important to share with him and what was not.

Even before the United States entered World War I, Mrs. Wilson had overseen her husband's workload.

These actions did not sit well with other government officials. Some people even referred to Mrs. Wilson as the "secret president." In 1920, President Wilson made a partial recovery from his **stroke**. He was able to finish his term.

The Wilsons left the White House in March 1921. They stayed in Washington, D.C. Mrs. Wilson continued to care for her husband. Then on February 3, 1924, Mr. Wilson died.

A Lasting Memory

After her husband's death, Mrs. Wilson worked to make sure people thought well of him. She carefully guarded his political papers. She also helped establish the Woodrow Wilson Birthplace Foundation in Staunton, Virginia. Today, it is the Woodrow Wilson Presidential Library.

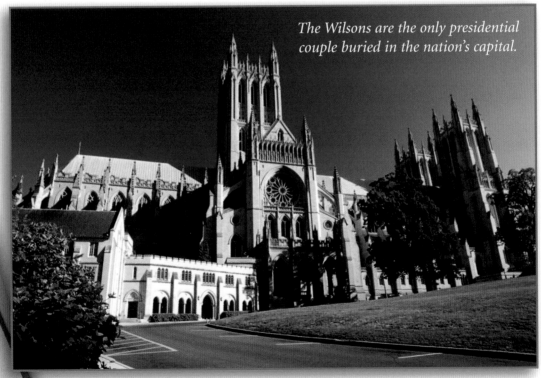

The Wilsons are the only presidential couple buried in the nation's capital.

The day Mrs. Wilson died, Mr. Wilson would have turned 105 years old.

Mrs. Wilson remained involved in Washington society for many years. In 1941, President Franklin D. Roosevelt asked Congress to declare war on Japan. This marked the entry of the United States into **World War II**. Mrs. Wilson sat with First Lady Eleanor Roosevelt during the speech. In 1961, Mrs. Wilson made her last public appearance. She attended the **inauguration** of President John F. Kennedy.

That year on December 28, Mrs. Wilson died at home. It was the same day as her husband's birthday. She was buried next to him in Washington National Cathedral in Washington, D.C.

Edith Wilson was First Lady for only part of her husband's presidency. Yet, she affected the United States like no other First Lady. She was criticized for this. However, she did what she believed was right. Today, Mrs. Wilson is remembered for her devotion to her husband and her country.

Timeline

1872	On October 15, Edith Bolling was born.
1887	Edith began attending Martha Washington College.
1889	Edith began attending Powell's School.
1895	On April 30, Edith married Norman Galt.
1903	Norman and Edith had a son, who died as an infant.
1908	In January, Norman Galt died.
1915	Edith met President Woodrow Wilson in March; on December 18, they married and she became First Lady.
1917	On April 6, the United States entered World War I; Mrs. Wilson began supporting the war effort.
1918	The Wilsons traveled to Europe at the end of World War I.
1919	On October 2, a stroke disabled President Wilson; Mrs. Wilson began acting as her husband's steward.
1921	In March, the Wilsons retired in Washington, D.C.
1924	Mr. Wilson died on February 3.
1961	On January 20, Mrs. Wilson made her last public appearance at John F. Kennedy's presidential inauguration; Mrs. Wilson died on December 28.

Did You Know?

Edith Wilson preferred to be called Mrs. Wilson.

In 1904, Mrs. Wilson purchased her own automobile. She became a frequent sight driving around Washington, D.C.

Mrs. Wilson was related to many U.S. presidential families. Her relatives included Presidents Thomas Jefferson, William H. Harrison, and Benjamin Harrison. She was also related to First Ladies Martha Washington and Letitia Tyler.

During World War I, Mrs. Wilson named more than 1,000 ships.

Mrs. Wilson was considered a possible vice presidential candidate for the 1928 election. That year, she spoke at the Democratic National Convention.

In 1939, Mrs. Wilson published a book about her life called *My Memoir*. She also approved the film *Wilson*, which was about President Wilson's life. The movie won five Academy Awards in 1945.

Glossary

amendment - a change to a country's constitution.

aristocrat - a member of a class of people having a high position in society by birth.

armistice - a pause in fighting brought about by an agreement between the two sides.

cabinet - a group of advisers chosen by the president to lead government departments.

civil war - a war between groups in the same country. The United States of America and the Confederate States of America fought a civil war from 1861 to 1865.

Constitution - the laws that govern the United States.

donate - to give.

honeymoon - a trip or a vacation taken by a newly married couple.

inauguration (ih-naw-gyuh-RAY-shuhn) - a ceremony in which a person is sworn into office.

neutral - not taking sides in a conflict.

newlywed - a person who just married.

paralyze - to cause a loss of motion or feeling in a part of the body.

steward - a person who manages the property, the finances, or the affairs of another person.

stroke - a sudden loss of consciousness, sensation, and voluntary motion. This attack of paralysis is caused by a rupture to a blood vessel of the brain, often caused by a blood clot.

World War I - from 1914 to 1918, fought in Europe. Great Britain, France, Russia, the United States, and their allies were on one side. Germany, Austria-Hungary, and their allies were on the other side. The war began when Archduke Ferdinand of Austria was assassinated. The United States joined the war in 1917 because Germany began attacking ships that weren't involved in the war.

World War II - from 1939 to 1945, fought in Europe, Asia, and Africa. Great Britain, France, the United States, the Soviet Union, and their allies were on one side. Germany, Italy, Japan, and their allies were on the other side.

Web Sites

To learn more about Edith Wilson, visit ABDO Publishing Company on the World Wide Web at **www.abdopublishing.com**. Web sites about Edith Wilson are featured on our Book Links page. These links are routinely monitored and updated to provide the most current information available.

Index